Wonders of the World

Written by Cathy Jones
Reading consultants: Christopher Collier and Alan Howe,
Bath Spa University, UK

First published by Parragon in 2012

Parragon
Queen Street House
4 Queen Street
Bath BA1 1HE, UK

ISBN 978-1-4454-6654-5
Printed in China

Discovery KIDS™

Wonders of the World

Bath • New York • Singapore • Hong Kong • Cologne • Delhi
Melbourne • Amsterdam • Johannesburg • Auckland • Shenzhen

Put on your 3D glasses and travel to the wonders of our world. They look so real you will want to reach out and touch them!

Parents' notes

This book is part of a series of non-fiction books designed to appeal to children learning to read.

Each book has been developed with the help of educational experts.

At the end of the book is a quiz to help your child remember the information and the meanings of some of the words and sentences. Difficult words, which appear in bold in the book, can be found in the glossary at the back. There is also an index.

Contents

The Grand Canyon

The Grand Canyon is the biggest **canyon** on the planet. It is a deep valley with steep sides. The Colorado River flows through it.

DISCOVERY FACT™

The Grand Canyon is 5,250 feet deep, 277 miles long, and up to 19 miles wide.

United States of America

The Grand Canyon

State of Arizona

Pacific Ocean

The Colorado River has worn through layers of rock. The oldest rocks at the bottom are almost 2 billion years old.

You can look down at the canyon through the glass floor of the Skywalk. The Skywalk juts over the canyon 4,000 feet above the river.

Canyon Skywalk

DISCOVERY FACT™

In 1901, a 63-year-old schoolteacher named Annie Edson Taylor became the first person to go over Niagara Falls in a wooden barrel—and live to tell the tale!

Niagara Falls

Niagara Falls lies between the United States of America and Canada.

The Niagara River flows around three islands and splits into three waterfalls. These are the Horseshoe Falls, American Falls, and Bridal Veil Falls.

A waterfall is made when a river flows over layers of rock and over time wears away the soft rock. A shelf of hard rock is left for the water to fall over.

About 100,000 cubic feet of water thunder over the Falls every second. That's about the same amount of water as in a large swimming pool.

Niagara Falls

The Sahara

The Sahara is the world's biggest hot **desert**. It covers most of northern Africa. It is one of the hottest and driest places on Earth. Very few plants and animals can live here.

Western Sahara
Algeria
Libya
Egypt
Mauritania
Sahara Desert
Mali
Niger
Chad
Sudan
Ethiopia
AFRICA

Camels are desert animals. The camel stores fat in its hump. It can live on the fat when it has no food or water.

An oasis is a pool of water in the desert. The water comes from deep under the ground. Plants and trees grow around it.

Camels

Oasis

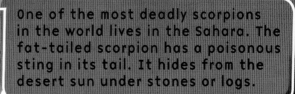

DISCOVERY FACT™

One of the most deadly scorpions in the world lives in the Sahara. The fat-tailed scorpion has a poisonous sting in its tail. It hides from the desert sun under stones or logs.

The Great Barrier Reef

The Great Barrier Reef is the largest living thing in the world. It is made up of tiny animals called coral polyps. Millions of these animals have joined together to make a reef that runs for over 1,200 miles.

Coral polyps are tiny sea animals that make their own skeletons of stone. Over hundreds of years, the skeletons build into coral **reefs**.

Indian Ocean

The Great Barrier Reef

AUSTRALIA

Indian Ocean

Coral reefs are home to thousands of other animals, from tiny clown fish to big green turtles.

The giant clam sticks itself to a spot on the reef and stays there for the rest of its life. Its shell can grow to 4 feet.

Giant clam

The Great Barrier Reef is the only living thing that can be seen from outer space.

13

Atlantic
Ocean

**Amazon
River**

**Amazon
Basin**

**SOUTH
AMERICA**

Pacific
Ocean

DISCOVERY FACT™

The jaguar is the third
largest wild cat. It is
well suited to the rain
forest and is even a
strong swimmer.

The Amazon rain forest

The Amazon **rain forest** is the biggest in the world. It covers an area the size of Australia. Over 180 inches of rain can fall in a year.

The tallest trees grow up to 130 feet tall. Their branches make a leafy blanket called the canopy. Brightly colored macaws, toucans, and parrots live here.

Macaws

The Amazon River flows through the rain forest. It begins in the Andes Mountains in Peru and flows through Brazil into the Atlantic Ocean.

The anaconda is the heaviest snake and spends a lot of its time in the water.

Anaconda

The Pyramids of Giza

The three great **pyramids** at Giza are over 4,500 years old. They were built for the **pharaohs** Khufu, his son Khafre, and his grandson Menkaure.

The Sphinx guards the way to Khafre's pyramid. It has the head of the king and the body of a lion.

These massive tombs were burial chambers, although no one has ever found a **mummy** inside them.

Over two million blocks of stone were needed to build Khufu's Great Pyramid.

Sphinx

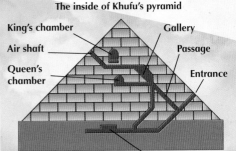

The inside of Khufu's pyramid

King's chamber

Gallery

Air shaft

Passage

Queen's chamber

Entrance

Underground chamber

DISCOVERY FACT™

The Great Pyramid was the world's tallest building for over 3,800 years.

Stonehenge

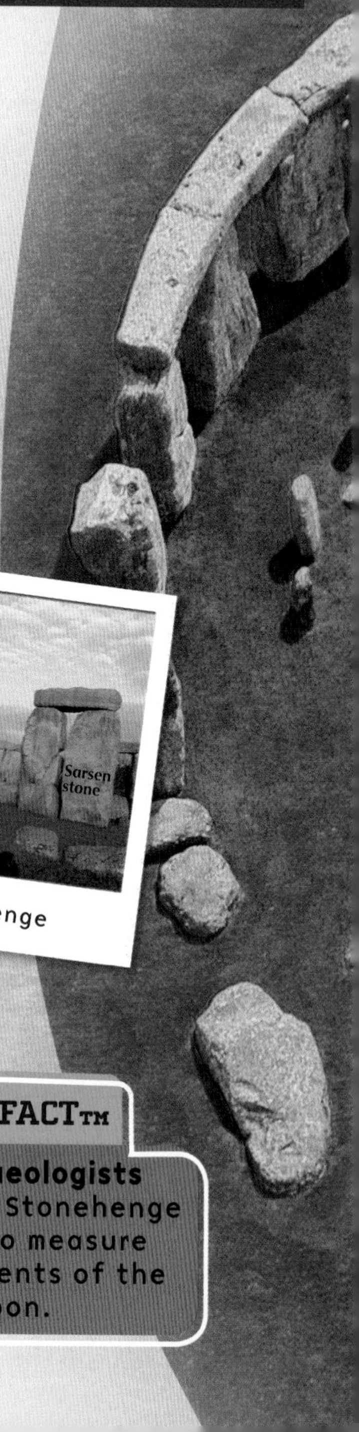

No one knows why this huge stone circle was built. It was probably built about 4,500 years ago at the end of the Stone Age. It may have been a temple where Celtic druids worshipped nature.

Pairs of stones, joined by a lintel, stand in two circles, one inside the other. The stones stand on a **henge**. A henge is a high bank circled by a ditch.

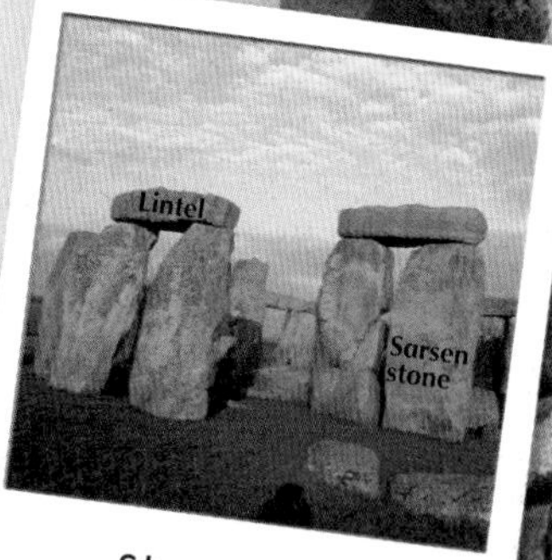

Lintel

Sarsen stone

Stonehenge

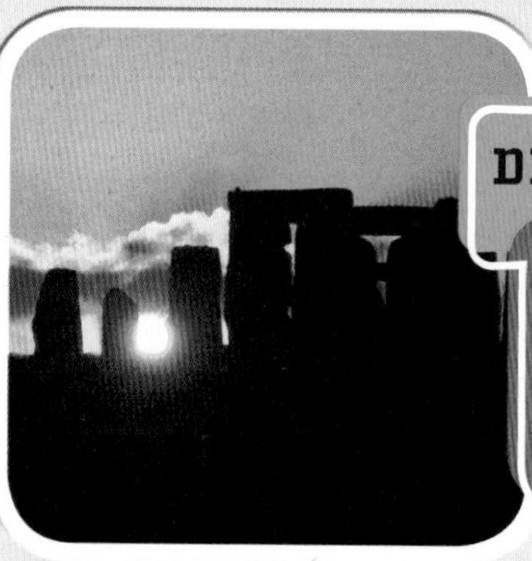

Atlantic
Ocean

**United
Kingdom**

●Stonehenge

19

The Great Wall of China

The Great Wall of China is the longest object made by humans in the world. It winds for more than 3,700 miles through mountains, deserts, and **marshes**.

Great Wall
China
Pacific Ocean
Indian Ocean

Over 2,000 years ago, Emperor Qin Shi Huangdi built the wall to stop enemies from invading from the north.

The Great Wall

The wall was wide enough for ten soldiers to march side by side.

Watchtowers were built all along the wall. Guards sent messages to the next watchtower using smoke signals.

DISCOVERY FACT™

The Chinese name for the wall is Wan-Li Wang-Qeng. It means 10,000-Li-Long-Wall (10,000 Li is about 3,000 miles).

The Colosseum

This open-air **amphitheater** in Rome was built in Roman times. Crowds packed the Colosseum to watch plays, pretend sea battles, and **gladiator** fights.

Inside the round building, rows of seats were arranged so that a crowd of 50,000 people could all have a good view of the action.

Gladiators were usually slaves or criminals who were trained to fight each other, or wild animals.

Animals and fighters waited in rooms and tunnels beneath the arena for their turn to fight.

Inside the Colosseum

When the Emperor Trajan won a battle in the year AD 107, he brought 11,000 animals and 10,000 gladiators to fight at the amphitheater over 123 days.

EUROPE

Italy

Rome

Mediterranean Sea

New York City

New York City has one of the most famous skylines in the world. It includes skyscrapers such as the Empire State Building and the Chrysler Building.

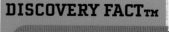

DISCOVERY FACT™

New York is known as the Big Apple. It was given its nickname by jazz musicians in the 1930s.

New York City is built on islands, including Manhattan and Staten Island. Part of it is also on the mainland.

Central Park

Central Park in Manhattan has a lake, a zoo, a theater, and an outdoor ice rink.

The Statue of Liberty was a gift from France in 1886 to mark 100 years of American independence.

Statue of Liberty

Quiz

Now try this quiz!
All the answers can be
found in this book.

How many soldiers could
march side by side along
the Great Wall of China?

a) Three

b) Five

c) Ten

What is New York's
nickname?

a) Big Apple

b) Big Orange

c) Big Peach

Where does the Amazon
River start?

a) Atlas Mountains

b) Andes Mountains

c) Rocky Mountains

What statue guards
the entrance to
Khafre's pyramid?

a) Mermaid
b) Centaur
c) Sphinx

Where is the Sahara?
a) Africa
b) Australia
c) South America

Which Roman
emperor won a battle
in the year AD 107?

a) Julius Caesar
b) Trajan
c) Hadrian

Glossary

Amphitheater
A circular theater with tiers of seating for the crowd surrounding an arena at the center.

Archaeologist
Someone who studies ancient remains to make sense of the past.

Canyon
A narrow, steep-sided valley, usually with a river at the bottom.

Desert
A dry, hot place where few plants and animals live.

Gladiator
A fighter in ancient Rome trained to fight other gladiators or wild animals.

Henge
An ancient large, raised, circular mound of earth, which is flat on top and surrounded by a ditch.

Marsh	An area of wet land.
Mummy	A dead body that has been preserved and wrapped in cloth.
Pharaoh	An ancient Egyptian ruler.
Pyramid	An ancient stone tomb with a square base and four triangular sides that reach a point at the top.
Rain forest	An area of forest that has a lot of rainfall and usually high temperatures.
Reef	A raised area of coral, rock, or sand just below the surface of the ocean.

Index

Acknowledgments

t=top, c=center, b=bottom, r=right, l=left

Cover: All images iStockphoto

p.1 John Heseltine/Corbis; p.3 John Heseltine/
Corbis; p.4 Comstock/Getty; p.6–7 Corbis,
p.6tl Corbis, p.7tr David Kadlubowski/Corbis;
p.8–9 Adam Booth/iStockphoto, p.9bl Vladimir
Mucibabic/iStockphoto; p.10–11 Jose Fuste Raga/
Corbis, p.11tl Antonela/Dreamstime, p.11b Frans
Lemmens/Getty; p.12–13 Comstock/Getty,
p.12b Comstock/Getty, p.13tl NASA; p.14-15 Niko
Guido/iStockphoto, p.15 cl Jeremy Woodhouse/
Getty, p.15bl Brian Kenney/Getty; p.16–17 Getty,
p.17tl Frederic Neema/Corbis, p.17bl Richard T.
Nowitz/Corbis; p.18–19 Jason Hawkes/Corbis,
p.18cr John Heseltine/Corbis, p.17bl Paul Prince/
LOOP IMAGES/Corbis; p.20–21 Corbis,
p.21cl Chen Xiaodong/Xinhua Press/Corbis,
p.21bl John Woodworth/Getty; p.22–23 John
Heseltine/Corbis, p.23tl After Antonio Niccolini/
Getty; p.24–25 Alan Schein Photography/Corbis,
p.24bl Sasha/Getty, p.25tl Rudy Sulgan/Corbis,
p.25cr Bill Ross/Corbis